Overheard while Shopping

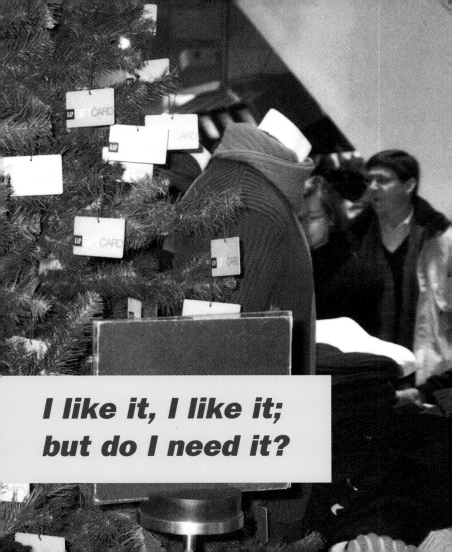

I like it, I like it; but do I need it?

There is a store I think you really would love; it's called K-Mart.

Overheard
while
Shopping

Judith Henry

UNIVERSE

First published in the United States of America in 2001
by UNIVERSE PUBLISHING
A Division of Rizzoli International Publications, Inc.
300 Park Avenue South
New York, NY 10010

The text in this book does not necessarily express the sentiments of the
pictured subjects.

2001 2002 2003 2004 2005 / 10 9 8 7 6 5 4 3 2 1

Design and photography by Judith Henry

Printed in Singapore

Library of Congress Control Number: 2001089895

Introduction

I always begin a shopping trip filled with hope. Perhaps this time I will find the pair of shoes or the shade of lipstick that will make me look fabulous. But since shopping for oneself is so intricately tied to self-image, it can be filled with anxiety. Why is the lighting in the store more revealing than at home? Why does everything look better on the hanger? Can I fit into this? Can I afford that? How does this really look on me? Will I be noticed? Will people stare? Do I really need it?

We shop to improve our appearance and status and keep ourselves in style. Shoppers are also intent on finding a bargain. That, too, is part of the challenge. For many it is an obsession and for others a necessary chore filled with dread. Lately, I have been watching and listening to the shoppers, and for me this is more fun than shopping.

From social outing to private ordeal, *Overheard while Shopping* is a reflection of my odyssey into the stores.

J.H.

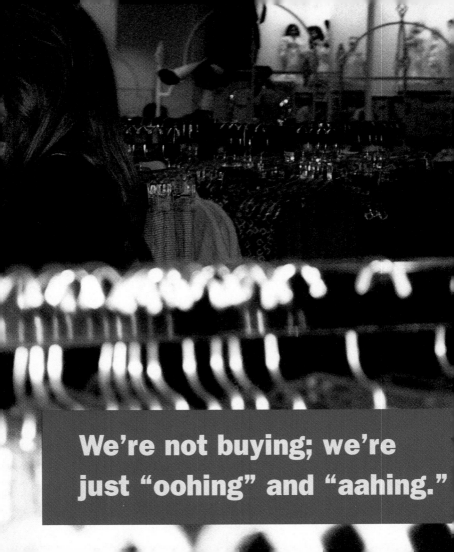

We're not buying; we're just "oohing" and "aahing."

I could almost afford this if I used all the parking quarters in my purse.

Let's get out of
here before we
buy something.

I need some lacy thongs to match my lacy thigh-highs.

I don't have a thing to do; I can spend money all day.

The shoes are definitely darker than the suit; do you think that's OK?

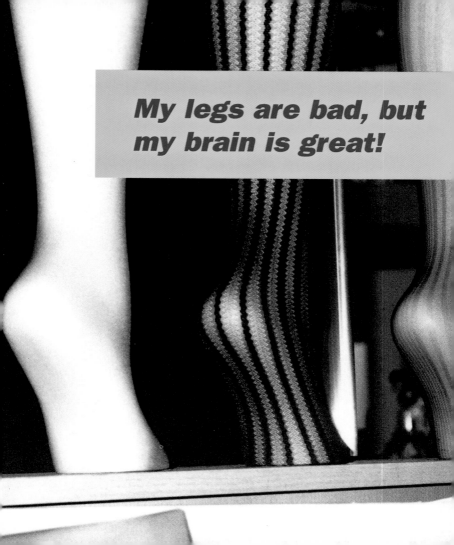

My legs are bad, but my brain is great!

I sort
of miss
being
rich.

I need to be the best-dressed one there tonight.

There are all kinds of green, Joan—Kelly, forest, mint, olive, and apple.

They're cool, but not as cool as the pair Tammy has.

Just let me know when it's time to pay; it's what I do best.

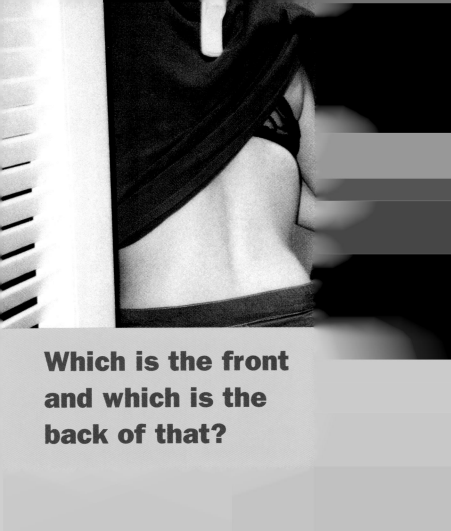

Which is the front and which is the back of that?

Could I get away with wearing this in the spring—after all, it's suede?

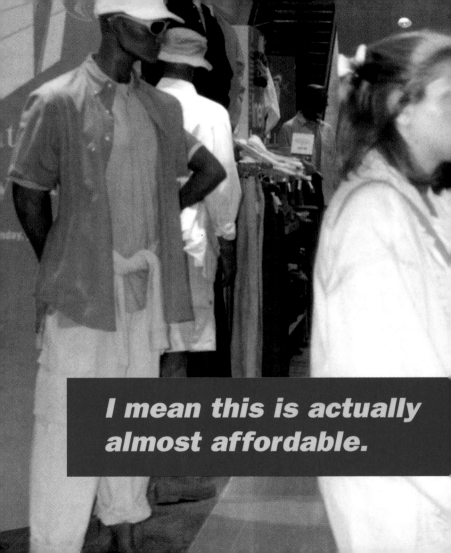

My daughter
tells me to
dress my age.

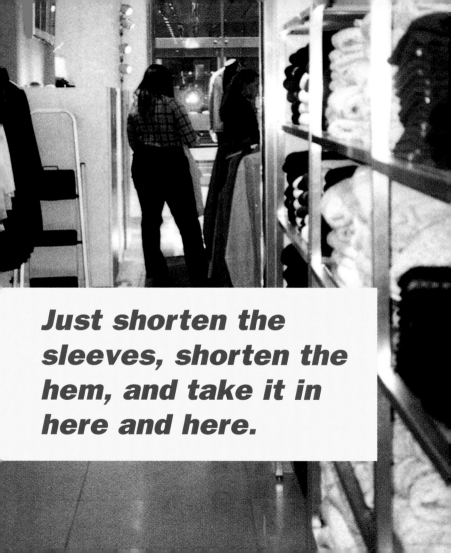

Just shorten the sleeves, shorten the hem, and take it in here and here.

I like this; it goes with my car.

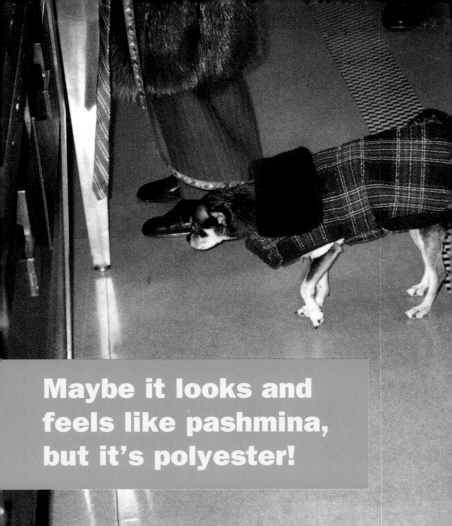

Maybe it looks and feels like pashmina, but it's polyester!

That was the
eighties;
try something
new.

Do you have anything
in an African animal
for around $500?

Harry would have a heart attack if I wore this.

I have a $25 gift certificate, and the cheapest thing here is more than $60.

ot becoming
u. Let me try

I'll buy anything just to end this ordeal.

Honey, you better sit down, I'm going to try on some shoes.

Is this ugly or cute?

Buy it, buy it, buy it.
So I can borrow it
from you.

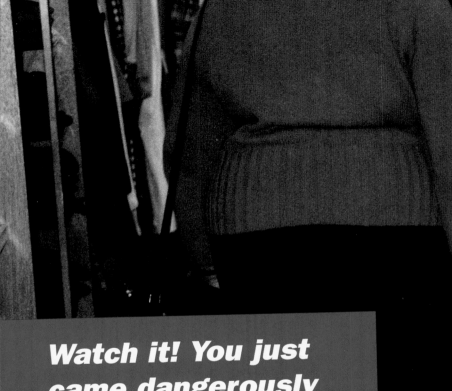

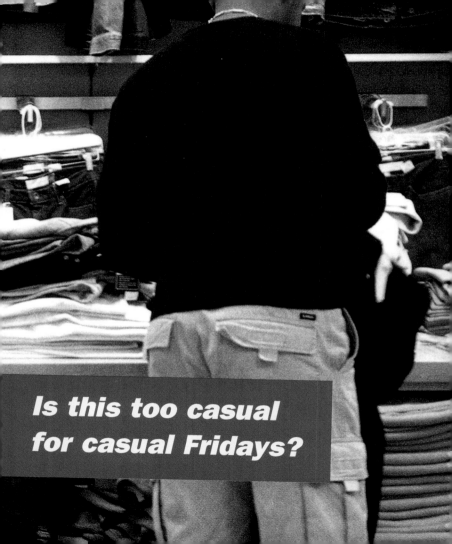

Is this too casual
for casual Fridays?

We just lost your mother again.

Mom, why can't I get something small? Look how small this is.

Do you know what it feels like when you've been shopping for four hours and haven't spent a cent?

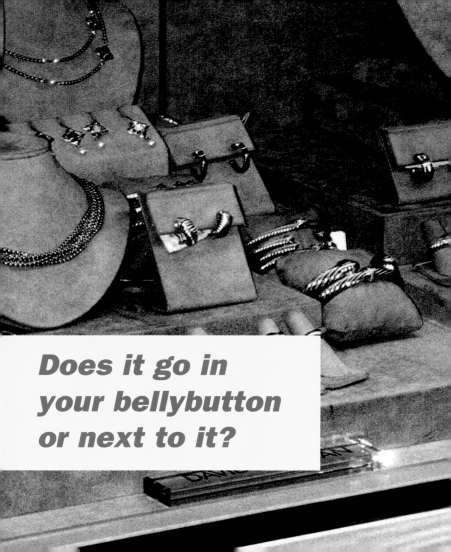

Does it go in
your bellybutton
or next to it?

*That diamond . . .
it's puny!*

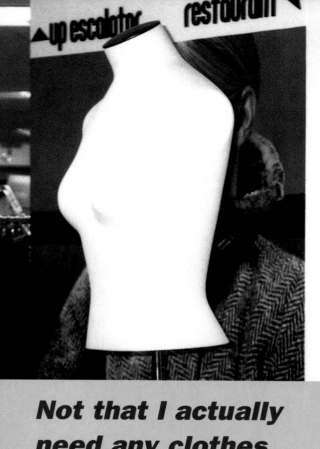

Not that I actually need any clothes.

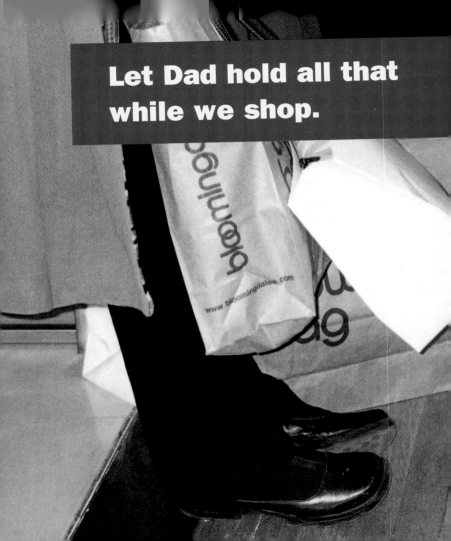

I could get contacts, but I like to look smart!

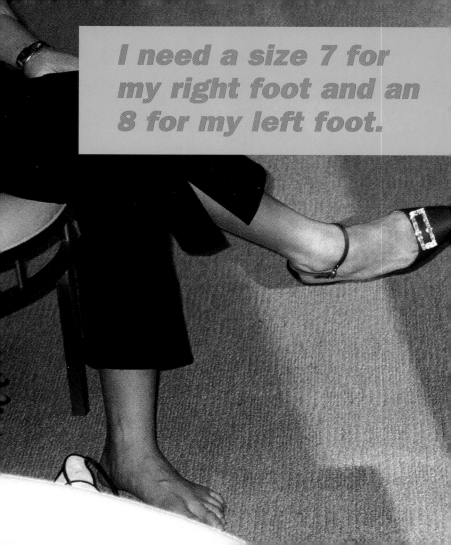

I need a size 7 for my right foot and an 8 for my left foot.

I have to go to the gym a few more times before I try that on.

Beauty

STĒ
AU

I need two shades of lipstick: wuss and cherish.

And we also have deep red, brandy kiss, teddy bear, and crushed berries.

Forget it. I am just going to buy everybody liquor for Christmas.

All you need is
a credit card.

You just can't dance through a store and think you're seeing it all.

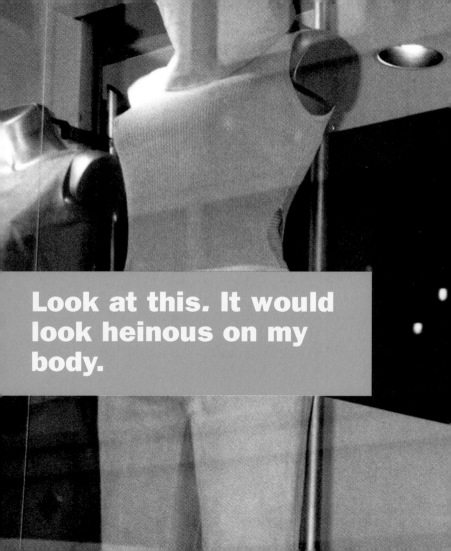

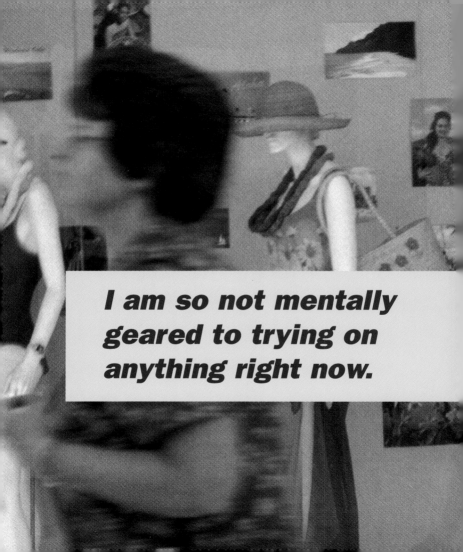

I am so not mentally geared to trying on anything right now.

I don't like
the white—
I mean I do,
but I don't.

They're expecting turquoise to make a comeback.

I don't know why you're taking black, with all these beautiful colors.

This is so cool. I don't care what it looks like on me.

I mean, seriously, you have to stop shopping.

About the Author

Judith Henry's art has been exhibited internationally in New York, Barcelona, Buenos Aires, and London among other places. She also designed works for The Museum of Modern Art, New York. In 1997 her book *Anonymous True Stories* was published. In 2000 Universe published her books, *Overheard at the Museum* and *Overheard at the Bookstore*. She lives in New York City.